The Revolutionary Swamp Fox

The Revolutionary
SWAMP
FOX

━ Idella Bodie

SANDLAPPER PUBLISHING CO., INC.
ORANGEBURG, SOUTH CAROLINA

Third Printing, 2002

Published by Sandlapper Publishing Co., Inc.
Orangeburg, South Carolina 29115

Manufactured in the United States of America

Library of Congress Cataloging-in-Publication Data

Bodie, Idella.
     The revolutionary Swamp Fox / by Idella Bodie.
          p.   cm.
     Includes bibliographical references.
     Summary: Describes the childhood, military service, and
     accomplishments of the Revolutionary War hero Francis
     Marion, known as the Swamp Fox.
       ISBN 0-87844-147-6
     1. Marion, Francis, 1732-1795—Juvenile literature. 2.
     Generals—United States—Biography—Juvenile literature.
     3. South Carolina—Militia—Biography—Juvenile literature.
     4. United States—History—Revolution, 1775-1783—
     Biography—Juvenile literature. [1. Marion, Francis, 1732-
     1795. 2. Generals. 3. United States—History—Revolution,
     1775-1783—Biography.]   I. Title.
     E207.M3B63   1999
     973.3'092—dc21
     [B]   98-54635
                                                        CIP
                                                         AC

FRANCIS MARION, hero of the American Revolution, was born in 1732 at Goatfield Plantation in St. John's Parish of Berkeley County, South Carolina. He was the youngest of six children. His French Huguenot parents, Gabriel and Esther Cordes Marion, moved to a plantation in Prince George, a parish on Winyah Bay near Georgetown, when Francis was about five. A great mysterious swamp lay at the edge of the Marion property.

In adulthood, Francis, like the other Marion children, owned a plantation on the Santee River. Francis's home was called Pond Bluff.

As a soldier, Francis Marion fought in a war against the Cherokee Indians in 1759 and in the Revolutionary War from 1775 to 1782. During the Revolution he earned the nickname of "Swamp Fox" by setting up camp on an island in the swamp and outfoxing the British soldiers with daring raids and clever disappearing acts into the swamp.

~ACKNOWLEDGEMENT~

I would like to honor Dr. Robert D. Bass for his exemplary biography of Francis Marion. Having been reared within a mile of Snow's Island where Marion and his men camped, Dr. Bass grew up on legends about him. Through the long years his research covered many sources, from the files of the Historical Commission of South Carolina to the unpublished correspondence of Lord Cornwallis located in the Public Record Office in London. Dr. Bass's Swamp Fox *won the American Revolution Round Table Award in 1959.*

To the Young Reader

History is made of stories remembered and passed on from generation to generation. Fortunately, historians have recorded a great deal of information on Francis Marion, known as the Swamp Fox of the American Revolution.

I chose slices from this vast collection of material that I felt would catch the spirit of Marion as a boy and soldier.

For your reading enjoyment I added conversation as it might have occurred based on facts. All factual material has been documented from earlier accounts, as noted in Sources Used.

If what you read here peaks your interest about this southern hero, you may want to locate books listed at the end of this brief story for further reading on Francis Marion and other heroes and heroines of the American Revolution.

Contents

Boyhood

The Soldier

The Revolutionary Swamp Fox

BOYHOOD

1.
A Problem

"Come help me, Francis." Job, one of Francis Marion's older brothers, sat on a stool in their barn corridor. He yanked shucks off ears of corn and stripped dried kernels from cobs with his bare hand.

Francis leaned into the barn stall and patted Star Bell, his favorite horse. Then he reached into Job's bucket for a handful of kernels and held them out to Star Bell.

"Hey, cut that out!" Job frowned. "Strip your own corn."

"I'll help you if you'll fight a cob war with me when we're through."

Job's hard kernels plinked into his bucket.

"Oh, all right," he said, "but get busy." He might as well give in, he thought. Francis always managed to outsmart him in one way or another,

even though he was younger and small for his age.

While he worked, Francis stuffed his pockets with cobs. Later he climbed into the corncrib, broke his cobs in half, and piled them at places he figured Job would come after him.

Before long, cobs zigzagged across the wide hallway of the barn. The brothers ducked and dodged and shouted.

At the other end of the hallway, their older brother Isaac plopped down on a bale of hay to mend the harness he carried. "If you hit me, you're gonna get ducked in the creek. I promise you."

Suddenly a voice from the barn door interrupted the fight. "Marse Fran—" It was Hannah, the Marions' cook. "Yo mama say you stop that chasing about this minute. You know it gone make you sick."

Francis fired one more strike for good measure. It hit Job broadside, and Francis leaped in joy. Then his happiness disappeared. He might as well stop, or his mother would be out to feel his forehead for sign of a fever or, worse still, rub his chest with that stinking goose grease and give him a dose of bitter medicine.

It was hard not to play war games when he

was always hearing talk of war. He'd overheard his father telling a neighbor that James Oglethorpe, the governor of the new colony of Georgia, was getting an army together to invade the Spanish in Florida.

Francis squinted, his dark serious eyes forming a frown. Oh, why did he have to be the only one of the six children to be so thin and pale and sickly? Even Esther, their only sister, didn't get sick the way he did. It wasn't fair—just plain, downright not fair.

2.
Lost!

The following morning, skies over the Marions' Low Country plantation were bright and clear.

"Son—" Francis's father turned toward him at the breakfast table. "One of the servants will row your mother, Esther, and me to the Videaus' plantation today. I'm counting on you to see that the lanterns are lighted at the creek landing. We'll probably need light by the time we return."

"And," his mother added, "be sure to take your tonic and lie down to rest after your noon meal. Hannah's making a meat pie, but don't eat too much. It might make you sick."

Later, at the landing, Francis stood watching the flat-bottomed boat shove off and move toward the flow of the Pee Dee River. He thought of the day he went with his father and their slave Prince to Charles Town.

The dugout the three traveled in was carved from the trunk of a cypress tree. As they started to leave shore, Job grabbed a big rock. "Here, Francis," he teased. "You'd better hold onto this so you won't blow out of the boat."

Francis had been too happy about the three-day trip to let Job make him angry by poking fun at his thinness.

As soon as his parents' boat was out of sight, Francis bridled Star Bell and threw a blanket over her back. Gabriel, the oldest of his four brothers, was supervising the field workers, and Francis saw no sign of Isaac, Ben, or Job.

Feeling a tug of guilt for slipping away

without telling anyone, he pressed his heels into Star Bell's sides and galloped toward the savannah with its tall sedge grass.

The air was sweet with honeysuckle blooms, and plump little thrush fluttered beneath scattered laurel bushes.

Star Bell's hoofs beat out a fast rhythm as they moved along. Suddenly, a wild turkey appeared out of nowhere in front of them, flapping its huge wings.

Star Bell reared. Francis yanked the reins, clutching the horse's mane to hang on until she calmed.

Soon they were moving among cattails and tall, slender reeds. The moldy smell of the swamp was strong; and before Francis knew it, they were in marshland thick with myrtle bushes. A lane of dark water stretched around cypress knees. Thick vines clung high in the tree branches, shutting out sunlight.

The swamp! They were in the swamp.

Marion reined in Star Bell. He hadn't meant to go all the way into the swamp.

Something bellowed. An alligator reared its long snout and snapped its jaws loudly. Star Bell made quick, restless movements. Francis froze.

In the dimness he watched the alligator raise its jagged back above the water and then sink down until only two dark knobs—its eyes—showed above the water's surface.

Star Bell continued to prance back and forth. How could Francis tell which way was out? They could go deeper and deeper into the swamp without knowing it.

How many times had his father cautioned

him about going into the swamp alone? "If the animals don't get you, you'll lose your way." Then he would add, "When you're older, Prince can teach you the ways of the swamp."

Francis knew that prince had grown up in the swamp. There wasn't anything he didn't know about the vast mysterious bog beyond their fields and savannahs.

In his fear Francis had held Star Bell's reins tightly. Now he loosened them, and Star Bell sloshed through pools of shallow water and wound past cherry laurel trees and dark holly bushes. A snake slithered over a knotted cypress root.

Francis bit his lip. He had to think. Even if he turned back now, he wouldn't be able to retrace their steps. The black, shallow water covered them. On the other hand, if Star Bell kept going this way and that, they would really

be lost.

"Whoa!" Francis pulled on the reins and looked up at the treetops. He couldn't see the sun well enough to get directions from it. Thick, dark tree branches hid it. The swamp looked the same in all directions.

Francis fought back fear. No one would know where he was. He had not meant to disobey his father.

While Francis sat, worrying, Star Bell grew impatient. She began a slow walk. Without being led by the reins, she headed through tangled roots onto high clumps of grass. Then she turned right, as if she knew where to go.

"Of course," Francis shouted. "I'll leave it to Star Bell. She'll take me home." He leaned forward and patted his horse's neck.

They brushed against long gray ropes of Spanish moss. Egrets and herons flew from branches over their heads. Alligators bellowed.

Finally, they were out of the swamp and moving across the savannah near the Marions' home.

Francis breathed a sigh of relief. Now he knew why his father had not wanted him to go into the swamp alone.

3.
A Narrow Escape

In spite of Francis's frightening experience in the swamp, he longed to return. He felt a fascination for the place.

One day while his parents and sister Esther sat on the veranda, Francis and Job ran about on the spacious lawn pretending they were lost in the swamp.

"For the last time, Francis," his mother called, "come sit on the steps, or I'll get your tonic."

Panting for breath, Francis chose the steps.

Esther looked up from her needlework. "All they can think about is the swamp. You'd think it was a beautiful place the way they act. But it's not. It's horrid and gloomy."

Francis couldn't believe his ears. How could Esther say such a thing? He would ask his father again if Prince could take him there—but he would wait until Esther was not around.

Before Francis found the right time to speak to his father about going to the swamp, the weather turned cold and damp. Francis became ill. As always, his mother remained ready with her bitter medicine. She also made him spend much time resting by the fire or in their small front bedroom.

Mr. Marion, noticing his son's quiet mood, tried to encourage him. "You will outgrow your fevers, Son," he said. "Your older brothers will have a hard time keeping up with you then."

Ben, the brother just above Job in age, added, "Francis is already the best horseman on the plantation."

Francis knew he looked frail, but he did have a wiry kind of strength. That helped him sit straight in the saddle.

One day when Francis was nine years old, he heard the good news. Prince would be taking him to the swamp.

As much as he liked Hannah's breakfasts of ham, cornbread, and fried sweet potatoes, he could hardly sit still long enough to eat.

Prince waited for him in a flat-bottomed boat at the creek landing.

Just as Francis stepped into the boat and laid his hatchet beside him, an owl hooted from a nearby magnolia.

"Lawsy me," Prince exclaimed. "I wish that owl hadn't hollered at us. It's bad luck for a owl to screech at you."

Francis held his breath. Surely Prince wasn't going to let a superstition keep them from going. "Awh, he wasn't hollering at us." Francis did his best to sound convincing. "Something in the tree probably scared him."

Prince rolled his eyes and stuck his paddle in the dark water. Soon they were moving through tall rushes. Prince laid the paddle in the bottom of the boat and picked up a long pole. With it he pushed off along the creek bottom, and they glided among swamp grasses.

After a while they left the reeds and grass behind and floated in a quiet lagoon.

Suddenly the crusty, jagged back of an alligator stuck up in front of the boat. Prince and Francis headed straight toward him. Just as they were almost on him, he disappeared. How many others lurked in the water? Francis shivered at the thought, even if the danger did excite him in a strange way.

A white wood ibis on the creek bank beat its wings and lifted off. A raccoon splashed nearby. "Look, Prince!" Francis pointed. "That animal looks like he has a mask on his face."

Prince paddled through water lilies with yellow blossoms. As they neared the shoreline, Francis spied a painted bunting. "That's the prettiest bird I've ever seen!" he called out.

"His wing broke, Marse Fran." Prince's voice sounded worried.

In a bound, Francis was out of the boat. Clutching his hatchet, he headed toward the colorful bird. It gave a pitiful cry and hopped a little way. Its broken wing trailed behind.

Something moved in the mud just beyond the bunting. A rattlesnake coiled, ready to strike! Its forked tongue darted in and out. The

tip of its tail moved back and
forth, making a buzzing rattle.
*The snake would kill
the bunting!*

"**Marse Fran!**"
Prince hollered, but
he was too late.
Francis had already swung his hatchet. The
blow cut off the snake's head.

Francis grabbed up the trembling bunting
and scrambled back into the boat.

"Marse Fran, don't you never do nothing
like that again. What your ma and pa say if they
learn I let you outa the boat in the swamp?"

Prince stepped out to retrieve the hatchet.
"Lawsy me, this snake got thirteen rattles on his
tail." He leaned down, cut the rattles off with his
knife, and stepped back into the boat. "Might as
well keep 'em for good luck."

Francis held the bird gently in his arms. "Now see, Prince, that owl hooting wasn't bad luck after all."

Prince shook his head. "Maybe not." But you sho tempted luck when you messed wid that rattlesnake. There's a wrong way and a right way to deal wid poison snakes, and you took the wrong."

Prince picked up the pole and pushed off from the creek bank to head homeward.

"Can I come back with you, Prince?"

"We'll have to ask your pa. You got a lot to learn about the swamp, Marse Fran."

At home Francis bound the bunting's wing with a soft cloth and put it in the tool shed. After a time the bird grew so tame it pecked rice grains from Francis's hand.

When the bird's wing healed, Francis took it to the edge of the swamp. He had known the time would come when he would have to let it go.

He could feel the bird's heart beating beneath its bright green feathers. With his own heart thumping, Francis moved as far out into the swamp as he dared. Then he lifted the bird as high as he could in the air and said, "Fly away home."

Perched on Francis's arm, the bunting made a start to fly. Instead, it drew back and fluttered its wings.

"Father said you wanted your freedom," Francis said, "but if you want to stay with me—"

At that moment the bunting lifted off. It sailed up and lit on the limb of a dead tree.

Francis stared so hard at the bird he did not realize the ground was moving beneath him.

4.
A Rescue

"Oh, no!" Francis cried aloud. "The ground isn't moving. I'm standing on a log—a floating log." He was in big trouble, drifting farther and farther out into the murky water.

In trying to get the bunting close to the swamp, he hadn't looked where he was stepping.

With all his might he struggled to keep from falling. How could he have been so stupid? How many times had he heard his father and Prince say, "Watch where you step in the swamp"?

The bank was too far to jump, and he didn't dare step in. Alligators liked shallow water.

"Isaac! Isaac!" He shouted at the top of his

lungs for his brother. Gabriel would be in the fields overseeing the workers, but surely Isaac could hear him. "Help! Quick!"

He called again and again. No answer. The log moved among pieces of rotten limbs and fallen twigs.

Suddenly the log began to roll. Francis held out his arms and struggled for balance.

Were alligators just waiting in the black water? His arms flailed until, finally, he steadied.

Then he saw a canebrake on the shoreline. If only—

To his surprise a strange face peered at him from the crowded growth of tall reeds. It was an Indian boy about his own age. Francis rarely saw an Indian. Most of them had left the area since the white men built homes and began to farm the land. He'd heard the ones who stayed were friendly. Was this one? He had to take that chance.

"Will you help me?" Francis called.

The Indian disappeared.

"Come back!" Francis called. And before he knew it, the Indian stood on the edge of the canebrake aiming his arrow at him.

Francis was about to yell "Don't shoot!" when an alligator between him and the bank slapped the water with its tail.

About that time Francis heard a *plunk*. He looked down to see an arrow stuck in his log. The arrow's quivering end had a vine tied to it.

"Grab vine!" the Indian shouted. "I pull you in."

Of course, Francis thought, he wasn't going to shoot me, and he didn't run away. He was getting the vine to send on his arrow.

Francis tried to brace himself as he caught

hold of the vine. Hand over hand the Indian tugged on the other end of the vine, pulling Francis toward shore. Francis clutched the vine tighter and tighter. At last the log ran up on the creek bank.

"Francis!" It was Isaac bursting through bay bushes. "You called me?"

"Yes." Francis was breathing hard. "But this Indian boy saved my life. I thought he was leaving me to the alligators, but he was cutting a strong vine for a rope to rescue me."

"What's your name?" Isaac asked.

The Indian pointed to the feather in his hair.

"It's Eagle Feather!" Francis exclaimed.

"Well, come with us, Eagle Feather," Isaac said. "We live nearby. Our father will want to reward you."

At home Mr. Marion thanked Eagle Feather and gave him a piece of red cloth and a small mirror. The boy looked in the mirror and laughed at himself.

The brothers walked with Eagle Feather back to the edge of the savannah where they called "Goodbye" and watched Francis's new friend disappear among the thick growth of the swampland.

5.
Friends

By the age of ten, as Mr. Marion predicted, Francis had outgrown his "fevers." He gained strength, and his muscles grew tougher; but he was still thin and pale and shorter than average. Even so, he was a fast runner and could climb the tallest trees on their farm. And, proudly, he had learned to shoot his father's musket.

Best of all, he could paddle or pole a boat through the swamp for many miles without getting tired. And he never got enough of the swamp. Although he was still not allowed to enter the wild, mysterious marsh alone, he went often with Prince when the servant hunted game for the family.

One day as Francis poled their boat through the swamp and Prince sat in the bow with his musket across his lap, Francis caught sight of Eagle Feather on high ground.

"Come with us!" Francis called out to him.

"No," Eagle Feather replied. "You come."

In moments Francis had poled the boat over and leaped out onto the grassy knoll.

"Marse Fran!" Prince yelled. "What your ma gone say? You know how she worry 'bout you and this swamp."

"Eagle Feather is our friend," Francis called back. "Father said so. Tell Mother I'll be home before dark."

Francis smiled and pointed to the little mirror Eagle Feather wore on a leather thong around his neck.

"The gift from my father?" Francis asked.

Eagle Feather nodded. "Bring me luck," he said.

"I wish I had Father's musket." Francis held up his empty hands. "But he won't allow me to shoot unless I'm with him."

"No need for gun." Eagle Feather checked the arrows in his quiver and slipped his loose bowstring into place at the end of his bow.

A short time later they were making their way around a huge mud flat. Eagle Feather stopped and pointed to a wide groove in the mud. "Where alligator drag his big body," he said.

Farther on they followed deer and bear tracks until they broke through laurel bushes to a sunlit pool.

Quickly Eagle Feather caught Francis's arm and pulled him back into the laurel thicket. He pointed toward a small lake where three deer drank.

The boys squatted down and peered through

the branches.

On the opposite shore herons stood high on their long legs, yellow like their bills. Turtles, sunning on logs, made plopping sounds as they slid into the water.

Francis was not ready to move on when Eagle Feather motioned to him.

Eagle Feather pointed out a dim trail. "Leads to bluff at river."

Francis strained to make out some kind of path under the spreading yellow jessamine. "How did you find it?"

"See two dead trees side by side?" Eagle Feather moved his hand from east to west. "Remember, path run this way."

In moments Eagle Feather was off, moving swiftly and quietly through the maze of bushes and trees.

Francis followed, amazed at the lightness of

his friend's step. He tried to place his feet where Eagle Feather's had been and listen carefully to all he said. With practice, he told himself, he could have a knowledge of the swamp like Eagle Feather.

They slipped through dark, shadowy places where thick leaves kept out light. Moss hung in long, ghostlike strands from cypress trees. In the dimness Francis caught sight of a snake slithering beneath a fallen tree.

"What would you do if a snake bit you?" Francis called.

Eagle Feather kept moving. At first Francis thought he had not heard his question. Then he saw his friend's head turn from side to side as if he looked for something.

Finally, he stopped, stooped down, and said, "See plant? It snakeroot. You dig root, chew, put on bite.

No, his parents need not worry about him as long as he was with Eagle Feather.

A tangle of muscadine vines twisted along the ground and up into the trees as far as they could see. Francis was wondering how they would get through when Eagle Feather caught a sturdy vine and swung over. He heaved the vine back to Francis for him to do the same.

Francis felt free and happy as he hurried after his friend toward a cleared area leading to a low bluff. A brightly colored wood duck with white head markings flew up from a clump of cattails.

"Path end here." Eagle Feather started up the knoll.

Standing on the rise of land, they could see the Pee Dee River.

"Can paddle boat up river from your house and go into swamp on high ground," Eagle

Feather told him.

Francis stood in amazement. He couldn't believe all he had learned from Eagle Feather in one afternoon. He was thinking of all the times yet to come when Eagle Feather said, "Go home now," and pointed to the sky. "Night come soon."

Moving in his same quiet, sure way, Eagle Feather led Francis back through the swamp and to the edge of the Marions' savannah.

"Thanks for teaching me about the swamp," Francis said as Eagle Feather turned to go.

"I teach more another day." As usual, Eagle Feather seemed to disappear in the shadows of the great swamp.

THE
SOLDIER

6.
Marion's Men

All through the colonies people were talking about separating from Great Britain. British officers began training soldiers who pledged allegiance to the King of England. They offered protection for all colonists who vowed to bear arms against fellow Americans. Marion and his brothers, who had grown into manhood, refused.

"You know I hate war," Marion told Job. "I don't want to fight again, but America must have liberty." The brothers sat under an oak at Pond Bluff, the plantation Francis Marion owned on the Santee River.

Remembering the sadness he had felt fighting the Cherokee Indians, Marion added,

"But as a member of the South Carolina Provincial Congress, I have no choice but to vote for war."

Congress did vote to fight, and Marion became a part of that fight. In 1776 he fought in the battle of Fort Moultrie and went on to defend the walled city of Charles Town with the Second South Carolina Regiment.

Unfortunately, Marion broke his ankle just before the Patriots were forced to surrender. He had to be returned home to Pond Bluff on a litter.

Eager to get back into the war, Marion did not wait for his ankle to heal properly. With his body servant Oscar's help, he mounted his horse and went about

recruiting men, black and white. From the area where he grew up, he formed his own regiment. Faithful Oscar traveled with him.

Those who joined Marion in the cause for freedom were not soldiers. They were simple backwoods farmers dressed in homespun, made of yarn in their homes on spinning wheels.

One hot August day these volunteers waited at Lynches Creek to meet their leader. They had ridden their own horses and brought hunting

muskets with bullets made from melted pewter plates.

"I hear he grew up on the Pee Dee River," one said. "I lived there myself as a boy, and I knew a Francis Marion. But he was a little scrawny fellow."

"That's the one," somebody else said. "You

might know Governor Rutledge would send us a runt."

As the men spoke, Marion and Oscar appeared through a growth of black gum trees.

"That's him," the first volunteer said under his breath. "Black-eyed and puny-looking just like he used to be. We'll never win a battle."

Marion, who had earned the title of colonel for courage in battle, halted his horse in front of the troops. He wore a close-fitting, bright crimson jacket. On his battered helmet was a silver crescent and the words "Liberty or Death," the mark of South Carolina's Second Regiment.

"Men," he said in a low voice, "we have the task of protecting the land and its people between the Santee and Pee Dee Rivers."

Marion nudged his horse forward several paces. Spanish moss streaming from oak branches formed a frame around him. "I love this land," he said. "If you feel that way too, we'll win the fight no matter how often we retreat." He bowed his head as if in deep thought, then turned his horse toward a lagoon along the creek's edge.

The men broke away, muttering to themselves and to each other.

"What's this about retreat?" one asked.

"I didn't volunteer to be a coward," another added. I came to fight." He raised his musket in the damp air. Others joined him.

Suddenly, almost like a shadow, Marion was among them again. If he heard their grumbling, he gave no sign of it.

"Men," he said, "follow me. I will show you our headquarters."

He lifted his canteen, took a gulp of the vinegar water he always carried, and they were off.

7.
Snow's Island

Marion headed deep into the swamp. All the while, he watched for familiar landmarks—dead pines standing tall like soldiers; a growth of small, hardy birch; the bare knobby knees of cypress trees anchored in dark water. At times like this he thought of Prince and Eagle Feather and the knowledge of the swamp he gained from them.

The horsemen rode on, twisting and turning through tangles of brambles and muscadine vines, sloshing through alligator infested waters and boggy marshland.

"I'll say one thing," a volunteer said to the rider nearest him, "he travels this swamp like he's got a map in his hand."

"I heard he learned it from an Indian," the other said.

Finally, the troop wound its way onto Snow's Island, a high, dry strip of land. Bringing their horses to a halt, the men grouped around their leader.

"Some of you know this area well," Marion said. "You've hunted these swamps. For others, I'll tell you the Pee Dee River runs along the east of us, the Lynches River along the north, and Clark's Creek along the south." Marion pointed in each direction as he spoke.

"We entered from the west," he went on. "That is the only way to get onto the island by foot or horseback. This is our hideout."

Marion dismounted and led his horse to graze along the high ridge running through the center of the island. Others did the same. A few still sat in their saddles, staring in amazement at the long, slender island hidden away in the vast swampland.

The men were used to living roughly, battling mosquitoes and sleeping on the ground during hunting trips. They gave no quarrel about their headquarters.

Still, some had doubts about the way Marion might act when they faced the enemy.

In his quiet way, Marion went about setting up guards and sending scouts in every direction to learn the location of Tory camps. Others built lean-tos to protect them from wind and rain and to store their scant supply of hominy grits, sweet potatoes, and corn.

One evening Marion perched on a stump eating roasted sweet potato Oscar had prepared. He rested his oak-bark plate on his knee and spoke to the men scattered around. "We'd better bed down soon. Before the sun's up, we'll surprise the Tory camp at Britton's Neck."

8.
Ambush

Stars still shone when Marion led his men to Britton's Neck, between the Little Pee Dee and Great Pee Dee Rivers.

Marion sat straight in his saddle. He wore his battered helmet. His sword dangled from his belt. Now and then he drew in his horse's reins and held a palm up to his men. It was his sign for silence. They must enter the enemy camp in the quiet manner of Indians.

In the camp, some men still slept; others cooked breakfast. Suddenly, Marion gave the order. Patriots pounced on Tories.

"The rebels are upon us!" one Tory shouted.

Half-dressed soldiers scrambled for the

woods. Marion's men charged after them.

"Colonel! Tories behind the camp are preparing to fight!" one Patriot warned.

Within moments, Tories fired from behind a crude fort. Bullets whizzed. A horse shrieked and fell. A fellow soldier scooped up the fallen man and swung him behind his saddle.

"Retreat, men!" Marion ordered.

His soldiers couldn't believe their ears.

"He *is* a coward!" one spat out, as he turned back to obey the order.

"The Tories are giving chase!" another shouted.

"I hate turning tail and running," still another yelled. "But orders are orders. I'll be a coward like the colonel."

Paying no attention to his men's faultfinding, Marion spurred his horse on, leading his troop to a different part of the swamp.

By the time Marion stopped in a dark area thick with hanging moss and the smell of decay, the horses breathed in noisy snorts.

The colonel motioned his men to draw close. "I know you hate to run from a fight." His black eyes flashed. "But remember, the man who runs away lives to fight another day."

In the distance they heard the British cavalry unit floundering through the swamp. Horses splashed across shallow ponds. Fallen sticks cracked.

"This place stinks!" a Tory shouted.

"Alligator!" another hollered.

A horse neighed and his rider cursed and yelled, " My horse is up to his knees in a bog!"

The Tories were getting close and time was running out. Marion spoke quickly. "Spread out, men, and keep hidden. Be prepared to ambush."

Men exchanged knowing looks. Did their little runt of a leader know what he was doing after all?

They moved as ordered, forming a circle

around the British soldiers. Lying in wait, they peered from behind thickets and Spanish moss.

Before long, handsome red uniforms shone in the dimness of the swamp. Marion shouted, "Close in!"

"It's a trap!" a Tory cried out. "Run!"

"Too late," others came back.

"Hold your fire!" Marion ordered.

Tories threw down their muskets.

"Collect their firearms and tie their hands," Marion commanded his men.

The colonel heard voices of his soldiers as they moved about him carrying out their orders. "Did you see how we tricked them?" one asked. "And not a man was lost," another said.

Marion had won the respect of his men. He knew his small, untrained brigade was no match for the British army. The only way to win was to outfox them. He had done exactly that.

9.
Daring Raids

News of Marion's victory spread. His men now knew their leader's tactics. They also knew he had their best interest at heart. He did not believe in unnecessary bloodshed. Still, some Patriots felt Marion should kill Tories, not take them prisoners.

Much plundering of homes and cruelty took

place over the land. Scouts reported that British Colonel Banastre Tarleton was allowing his men to burn homes, run off cattle, and shoot Patriots who tried to defend their property.

Such reports made Marion more determined than ever to rid America of its royal government. He increased the number of hit-and-run attacks.

The colonel waked his men before sunrise. No bugles blew or drums sounded like those in regular regiments. Only birds saluted them from mossy trees while they fed their horses and squatted to eat a quick meal of sidemeat and cornbread.

Sneaking up on Tory camps, Marion's men struck again and again, sometimes hovering close to camps to raid Tory supply wagons. Once discovered, the chase was on until the small brigade disappeared into the mist of the swamp. There they lurked in dark marshes waiting to ambush the enemy.

One raid, however, did not go as planned. When Marion found Shepherd's Ferry on Black Mingo Creek well guarded, he moved north to the only bridge in the area. As he led his men across, loose wooden planks echoed the clatter of horse's hoofs like thunder in the night.

A warning musket shot sounded from the British camp. Lights went out in the farmhouse used as British headquarters. There was no turning back.

"They are ready and waiting for us," Marion said. "Pass the word."

In their usual manner of attack, Marion scattered his men, sending some to the right and others to the left. He waited with his remaining men outside the camp.

Tories, hidden on the edge of a field, opened fire, and the battle was on. Marion's men fought with muskets and homemade swords.

At last, Tories began to retreat but not before both sides suffered heavy losses. This was a sad occasion. From that time on, Marion laid blankets on wooden bridges to muffle their horses' hoofs.

Sometimes Marion's little band harassed Tory camps late at night. The Patriots rode up and down at a distance, whooping like a Cherokee war party to unnerve the enemy. Besides, scare tactics saved ammunition that was always scarce.

When Marion was successful in his raids, he sent food to his soldiers' families. He also let his men go to their homes from time to time to check on their families and crops. After all, they were unpaid volunteers.

One day a scout brought a message to camp: "Colonel Banastre Tarleton has been ordered to wipe out General Marion and his so-called brigade."

Marion listened to the threat and took a sip of his vinegar water. "I'm pleased," he remarked, "especially now that we have equipped ourselves with fine weapons and supplies furnished by the Tories themselves."

The next time Marion's men swooped down on Tarleton's camp like a swarm of yellow jackets, the Tory army set out after them.

After a seven-hour chase, one of Tarleton's officers asked, "Shall we keep after them, Sir?"

Tarleton shook his head. "The devil himself couldn't catch that fox once he's in the swamp."

Hearing the story, Patriots gave Marion the nickname "Swamp Fox."

The commander of the Southern Continental Army, General Horatio Gates, was not impressed with the swarthy little Huguenot with a limp and his band of ragged men. But when General Nathanael Greene replaced Gates as commander, he quickly enlisted Marion's help.

"I have not the honor of your acquaintance," Greene wrote, "but am no stranger to your character and merit."

Actually, General Greene's tactics were similar to Marion's in the use of guerrilla warfare. In short order, Greene asked Marion to lead an attack on British-held Georgetown. He sent Colonel Harry Lee (called Light-Horse Harry) to help him.

Lee finally found Marion on Snow's Island, quietly sipping his usual drink. Pale, eagle-nosed, and poorly dressed, Marion was quite a contrast to handsome Lee in his green jacket, white breeches, and plumed leather helmet.

Lee was a stately Virginian and highly educated with polished manners. Marion, a backwoodsman, had little formal education and was more casual in his manner.

In spite of their differences, the officers learned to work together and grew to respect each other. In fact, at one point Lee placed himself under Marion's command.

When Lee received orders to report elsewhere, Marion continued to raid British supply lines, Indian style, and send provisions to Greene's army. He also kept up his spy networking and raids along the Low Country tidewater and marshes, the land he knew and loved best.

When General Greene returned to South Carolina, he honored Marion's brigade by making them a part of the American Continental Army. In many ways this did not suit Marion's men. They had been allowed to slip off to see about their homes and family. As a result of this change, some of Marion's militiamen dropped out of army life.

Marion, too, had liked making his own plans, but now he moved only when ordered to do so. Nevertheless, he remained faithful during many more battles until the war ended.

10.
Return Home

In December 1782 Marion called together the men who had remained with him. They gathered near a cedar grove at Fair Lawn Plantation, where they sometimes camped. Although ragged and hungry, they were now free to find their way home.

Marion faced his men in the same patched and faded crimson jacket, black pants, and dented helmet he wore the first day they gathered.

For a while they all sat in silence, the Patriot soldiers awaiting the words of their honored leader.

Marion's black eyes swept down the line of

tired, thin faces. "Men," he said, "the fighting is over. Go back to your farms and families. May God bless you for the fine deeds you have done." With Oscar by his side, Marion turned and rode off among the cedar trees.

The soldiers remained, talking. "He was the best," one said. "Always thinking of us first."

"Remember the time we built that tower of logs and moved it up to Fort Watson at night?" another asked.

"Yeah," a soldier answered, laughing. "Were they surprised when we shot down on them?"

"How about the way we captured the

house—the one that belonged to that Motte lady and the British took it for a fort? I can still see those flaming arrows going up in the air."

"Or when we freed the prisoners the British were taking from Camden to Charles Town?"

"Nothing could ever top the way we ambushed those Tories in the swamp."

All agreeing on the victories shared, they headed home—some on horseback, others on foot.

Marion knew British soldiers had camped on and raided his homeland, but the conditions he found on his return were much worse than he imagined. Pond Bluff, the plantation he had purchased as a young man, was in ruin. The house had been plundered and partly burned. Cattle had been driven off, horses and farm equipment taken.

Since Marion had no pay from his service in the militia, he bought animals, tools, and seed on credit to start again. With the same determination that kept him fighting, he began to make his home livable. The few faithful servants who remained helped restore Pond Bluff.

Many honors came to Marion for his patriotism and leadership in his country's fight for freedom. He was awarded the rank of brigadier general. Congress honored him for wise and gallant conduct in defending his country, especially in the Battle of Eutaw Springs.

For as long as he would allow them to do so, voters kept him serving in the state senate. He also served as a delegate to the convention where he helped write the Constitution of South Carolina.

In 1786 Marion married Mary Esther Videau whom he had known since childhood. They built a simple, one-story house of cypress on Pond Bluff Plantation. Marion always welcomed his comrades of war, greeting them in his battered helmet.

Marion never lost his love for roaming on horseback. On occasion he and Mary, accompanied by Oscar, packed camping gear and set out along the Santee River. On their way they visited old friends.

The cruelty of war had always worried this gentle man. He never allowed his soldiers to plunder or destroy property. Now he forgave Tories who were willing to swear allegiance to America.

Years of daily warfare and nights in the swamp affected Marion's health, which had been so frail as a child. His physical condition gradually grew worse. On his deathbed he told Mary, "I can truthfully say that I have never intentionally wronged any man."

Francis Marion died February 27, 1795, at the age of sixty-three. He is buried in the family cemetery on his brother Gabriel's plantation at Belle Isle.

The remains of Marion's Pond Bluff home now lie under Lake Marion, a man-made lake that supplies hydroelectric power to a large part of South Carolina.

Over the past two centuries, parents have named their sons Francis Marion. Cities and counties across our country, as well as a national forest, bear his name.

This scrawny little Hugenot and his band of ragged men were not aware they were earning a shining place in legend and history of America's war for liberty. Through song, tales, and poetry their story is told. Francis Marion is truly a South Carolina native who belongs to the nation.

Song of Marion's Men

Our band is few, but true and tried,
    Our leader frank and bold;
The British soldier trembles
    When Marion's name is told.
Our fortress is the good green wood,
    Our tent the cypress tree;
We know the forest round us
    As seamen know the sea.
We know its walls of thorny vines,
    Its glades of reedy grass;
Its safe and silent islands
    Within the dark morass.

Woe to the English soldiery
    That little dread us near!
On them shall light at midnight
    A strange and sudden fear;
When, waking to their tents on fire,
    They grasp their arms in vain,
And they who stand to face us
    Are beat to earth again;

And they who fly in terror deem
    A might host behind,
And hear the tramp of thousands
    Upon the hollow wind.

Then sweet the hour that brings release
    From danger and from toil;
We talk the battle over,
    And share the battle's spoil;
The woodland rings with laugh and shout,
    As if a hunt were up,
And woodland flowers are gather'd
    To crown the soldier's cup.
With merry songs we mock the wind
    That in the pine-top grieves,
And slumber long and sweetly
    on beds of oaken leaves.

Well knows the fair and friendly moon
    The band that Marion leads—
The glitter of their rifles,
    The scampering of their steeds.
'Tis life to guide the fiery barb
    Across the moonlight plain;

'Tis life to feel the night-wind
    That lifts his tossing mane.
A moment in the British camp—
    A moment—and away
Back to the pathless forest,
    Before the peep of day.

Grave men there are by broad Santee,
    Grave men with hoary hairs,
Their hearts are all with Marion,
    For Marion are their prayers.
And lovely ladies greet our band
    With kindest welcoming,
With smiles like those of summer,
    And tears like those of spring.
For them we wear these trusty arms,
    And lay them down no more,
Till we have driven the Briton
    Forever from our shore.

—William Cullen Bryant

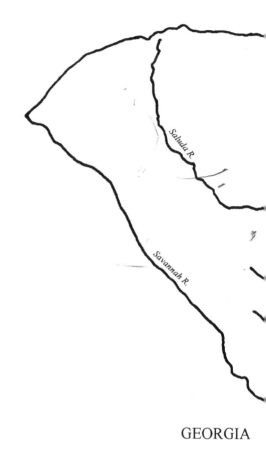

GEORGIA

South
Carolina

Words Needed for Understanding

allegiance	loyalty to a person, group, or country
ambush	a war tactic in which persons in hiding make a surprise attack on the enemy
backwoods	remote wooded area
bed down	prepare and use a sleeping place
bog	wet, spongy ground made up of decayed plants
brambles	prickly shrubs or vines
breeches	trousers reaching the knees
brigade	group of military persons
bunting	a bird related to the finch family
canebrake	crowded growth of cane plants
canteen	small container for carrying drinking water

cavalry	combat troops mounted on horses
comrades	persons who share the same interests and activities
Continental	relating to a soldier of the American colonies during the Revolutionary War
corncrib	a structure with openings for fresh air used to store ears of corn
corridor	a long passageway
cypress knees	knee-like, woody growths low on the trunks of cypress trees
dugout	a boat or canoe hollowed out of a log
fascination	a strong attraction to some thing or person
flail	swing one's arms about wildly
frail	physically weak
gallant	brave and noble

game	wild birds or animals hunted for food
guerrilla warfare	military actions carried out by small groups under cover, designed to harass and weaken the enemy
harass	worry or torment others
homespun	coarse, loosely woven cloth made of yarn at home on a spinning wheel
Huguenot	French Protestant of the sixteenth or seventeenth century
hydroelectric power	electricity produced by waterpower
knoll	small hill
lagoon	a shallow lake connected to a larger body of water
landmark	any fixed object, like a tree or building, that serves to show direction

lean-to	a temporary shelter with a slanting roof, supported on one side
legend	a story, believed to have historical basis, that passed orally from generation to generation
litter	a stretcher on which a sick or wounded person is carried
lurked	stay hidden, ready to attack
Marse	a title used by a servant in addressing white men and boys rather than using Mister or Master
marsh	low-lying watery land
militia	a volunteer group of soldiers, usually made up of ordinary citizens
murky	dark
muscadine	a kind of wild grape
musket	a long-barreled firearm

outfox	act smarter than the enemy
Patriot	one who loves and supports his country; American colonist who fought for freedom
pewter	a dull gray metal made by mixing tin with one or more other metals
plundering	taking by force, as in war
provisions	food and other supplies gathered and stored for future needs
predict	say something will come true
rebel	a person who refuses to be controlled
regiment	a military unit
retreat	withdraw when faced with danger
runt	a person or animal of small size
savannah	open, level grassland
scout	a person sent out to spy on the enemy

scrawny	skinny and bony
sidemeat	bacon or salt-cured pork
spinning wheel	wheel-driven machine that spins yarn, operated by hand
spy networking	the act of watching enemy action and connecting with others doing the same
snakeroot	a plant used as a medicine on snakebites
superstition	a belief based on fear or ignorance
swamp	wet, spongy ground sometimes covered with water (Swamps have both wet forests with trees and shrubs and grassy marshland.)
swarthy	having a dark complexion
tactics	plans of action in war
tonic	medicine to increase body strength

Tory   a person living in the colonies who
                gave allegiance to the king of England
                during the American Revolution

troop   a group of soldiers

veranda   an open porch, usually with a roof

wiry   thin and strong like wire

Things to Do and Talk About

1. This book uses the word Tory to stand for a person who favored Great Britain in the Revolution. (The word Tory was taken from one of the political parties in England.) The colonists who sided with the British preferred to be called Loyalists. Why do you think this is so?

2. American colonists who fought for freedom from British rule called themselves Patriots. (They were also called Whigs, taken from a political party in England who wanted law reform.) The British and the Tories called the Patriots rebels. Do you think the word rebel fits? Explain.

3. Describe how Marion's men differed from other soldier units fighting in the Low Country.

4. As a boy Francis Marion gained much knowledge of the swamp. How did he use this knowledge as a soldier in the Revolution?

5. The little town of Jacksonboro near Charles Town played a big part in the Revolutionary War. Can you find out what this was?

6. Francis Marion and Nathanael Greene used a kind of guerrilla warfare. Can you explain what is meant by "guerrilla" warfare and why it would confuse the enemy?

7. From what this biography says about Francis Marion and Henry Lee, compare and contrast them in appearance and personalities.

8. Why do you think Marion's men came to feel such admiration for him?

9. This story says Marion fought in the battle of Fort Moultrie. Can you tell the story of Sergeant William Jasper who became a hero in that battle?

10. A city in South Carolina and one in Ohio are named for Marion, as well as counties in South Carolina and Oregon. Find as many places as you can that are named for this Revolutionary War hero.

11. Draw a map of South Carolina. Put in rivers and places mentioned in this story.

12. Form small groups in your classroom and write plays based on the chapters in this book. Besides writers, actors, and actresses, you will need stage di-

rectors and costume designers. Perform your plays before other classes.

13. Ask your teacher or a parent to read you the poem "Song of Marion's Men" located at the end of this biography. Listen carefully to the ballad rhythm as the story of Marion and his men is told in verse.

14. It was said Patriots drank coffee during the Revolution and called it "Liberty Tea." Why do you think they did this? What part did tea play in the war? Can you find out what the Boston Tea Party was?

Sources Used

Bass, Robert D. *Swamp Fox*. Orangeburg, SC: Sandlapper Publishing Company, Inc, 1974.

Boddie, William Willis. *History of Williamsburg*. Columbia, SC: State Printing Company, 1923.

Burney, Eugenia. *Colonial Histories: South Carolina*. Camden, NJ: Thomas Nelson, Inc., 1970.

Dictionary of American Biography, Volume XII. New York: Charles Scribners Sons, 1933.

Hennig, Helen Kohn. *Great South Carolinians, Vol. 1*. Chapel Hill, NC: University of North Carolina Press, 1940.

Hilborn, Nat and Sam. *Battleground of Freedom: South Carolina in the Revolution*. Columbia, SC: Sandlapper Press, Inc., 1970.

Holbrook, Stewart H. *The Swamp Fox of the Revolution*. New York: Random House, 1959.

Moultrie, William. *Memoirs of the American Revolution, Volume I*. New York: Arno Press, 1968.

Osborne, Anne Riggs. *The South Carolina Story.* Orangeburg, SC: Sandlapper Publishing Company, Inc., 1988.

Ripley, Warren. *Battleground: South Carolina in the Revolution.* Charleston, SC: Post-Courier Books, 1983.

Steele, William O. *Francis Marion: Young Swamp Fox.* New York: Bobbs-Merrill Company, Inc., 1962.

Wallace, David Duncan. *South Carolina: A Short History, 1520-1948.* Columbia, SC: University of South Carolina Press, 1966.

About the Author

Idella Bodie was born in Ridge Spring, South Carolina. She received her degree in English from Columbia College and taught high school English and creative writing for thirty-one years. She has been writing books for young readers since 1971.

Mrs. Bodie lives in Aiken with her husband Jim. In her spare time, she enjoys reading, gardening, and traveling.

Books by Idella Bodie

HEROES AND HEROINES OF THE AMERICAN REVOLUTION

Brave Black Patriots
The Courageous Patriot
The Fighting Gamecock
The Man Who Loved the Flag
Quaker Commander
The Secret Message
Spunky Revolutionary War Heroine

OTHERS

Carolina Girl: A Writer's Beginning
Ghost in the Capitol
Ghost Tales for Retelling
A Hunt for Life's Extras: The Story of Archibald Rutledge
The Mystery of Edisto Island
The Mystery of the Pirate's Treasure
The Secret of Telfair Inn
South Carolina Women
Stranded!
Trouble at Star Fort
Whopper